Free Verse Editions
Edited by Jon Thompson

Also by Jean Gallagher

Stubborn
Winner of the FIELD Prize

This Minute
Winner of the Poets Out Loud Prize

Start

RIVERMOUTH SHOUTING

Jean Gallagher

Parlor Press
Anderson, South Carolina
www.parlorpress.com

Parlor Press LLC, Anderson, South Carolina, 29621

Library of Congress Cataloging-in-Publication Data

Names: Gallagher, Jean, 1962- author
Title: Rivermouth shouting / Jean Gallagher.
Description: Anderson, South Carolina : Parlor Press, 2026. | Series: Free verse
    editions | Summary: "The two sequences of poems in Rivermouth Shouting
    explore the permeable, unfixed nature of embodiment. "To Noah, From
    Wife" considers the play of boundaries in a long marriage after the looding
    of everything. Through a prehistory of early made objects and the voices of
    Homer's soldiers and civilians at Troy, "Rivermouth Shouting" traces the
    evolution and unmaking of the idea of the stable, separate body, as notions
    of fixity and boundary are built (by skin, armor, ideation) and unbuilt (by
    wounding, dying, and practices of unselfing and dereifying)"-- Provided by
    publisher.
Identifiers: LCCN 2025044826 (print) | LCCN 2025044827 (ebook) |
    ISBN 9781643175591 paperback | ISBN 9781643175607 pdf | ISBN
    9781643175614 epub
Subjects: LCGFT: Poetry
Classification: LCC PS3607.A415435 R58 2026 (print) | LCC PS3607.
    A415435 (ebook) | DDC 811/.6--dc23/eng/20251215
LC record available at https://lccn.loc.gov/2025044826
LC ebook record available at https://lccn.loc.gov/2025044827

2 3 4 5

Cover image: Daniel Riccuito, *Transfiguration*, 2025, concentrated watercolor
    on velour paper, 9 x 12 in.
Cover image photograph by Maggie Birdsell.
Book design by David Blakesley.

Parlor Press, LLC is an independent publisher of scholarly and trade titles in
print and multimedia formats. This book is available in paperback and ebook
formats from Parlor Press on the World Wide Web at https://www.parlorpress.
com or through online and brick-and-mortar bookstores. For submission
information or to find out about Parlor Press publications, write to Parlor
Press, 3015 Brackenberry Drive, Anderson, South Carolina, 29621, or email
editor@parlorpress.com.

Contents

Contents

There is a study of water telling of water.
—Eihei Dogen

Rivermouth Shouting

To: Noah/From: Wife

I want a nice little boat made out of ocean.
— Tom Verlaine

Subject: Ark Ideation and Prototyping

I was sitting there quietly modeling it out of code
and light, the little speakers in my fingers
saying *let there be* so loud
they didn't hear the blink that says *let
there not*. Sure, the light was bloodtied
to us in the early furnaces. In
the course of something else burning we
became ourselves. Insofar as it
disintegrates, it is called the world.

Subject: Causes and Effects

Of course I was the one who drowned the old
world. I'd wanted it emptied-slash-
filled by an element essential to life but, whoa,
fatal in large quantity. I'd wanted less,
concentrated. But here was math of it: 2 +
idea = the 10K things. Hence
the box built to float over what
I'd killed, and everyone got in. If
"everyone" = a representative sample of
the total zoo, which rides with us now
fulltime. Nights, the animals sleep and we
can grab a drink up on deck under
the tarp. It'll rain a while yet.
The 2's turn in their beds and the black bird
and the white wait for their chance to bring a little
branched something--evidence of *else*—
back before never anymore coming home.

Subject: Ark Negative

We met really as the rocking of things there,
no trace of us having gone all the way in.

Subject: Glass Box

Brought back that glass box of ocean,
the glass a kind of ocean too but slower.
The green world was strange, nothing holy,
lots of space. When I looked too fast
at things they looked like ocean still, *my
eyesight* a splash of salt water
I didn't actually own. The last
thing the boat/god said was *study
the moment when water sees water*. We
are married as the ocean is to its
glass self, is, is not, is.

Subject: The Animals Go Out

The animals do pretty much what
they like now. Terrifying, watch-
ing them hoof it, contained by what

anymore but a sky like a dry-
erase board and they the dry-
erasable skidmarks. The animals are slipping by

and staying out late and coming home high
as little paper kites that trust the sky
like they were rain. As they are. As am I.

Subject: What Wd It Be To Be Water
(We Are Water Divided)

after Marie Ponsot

We look at each other over the floodplain till one of us says *what*
?. Then the other answers, *what*. This wd
be a game we've played forever. It
is younger only than a similar game called *you*. Don't be
gone long, darling. I need to
reassemble all the pairs to be
parted by the water
of themselves. But for now we
can be the two boats we are
always building out of water.
I don't know if you'd call that *un-* or *-divided*.

Subject: Gangway

Took a walk in the recession today, stirred
up a few of those liquid metal
ideas shining in the mud, the mud too
all shine, sillioned by the gangway of things.

Rivermouth Shouting

Prologue: Early Things

Hand Axe

I kept on hitting *this*
                    this
                    this
the single
hard event
pure *each*.

                                    What chip
                        of it lodged
                            in my mind   *I could have*
                                                            something
                                                                            just like this
                                                        again.

That first idea   faulty
template   bright
unhappiness   *more   more*
                    of the same.

Bead

Why did it take so long to say it
      I am also that
to circle this self with a harder
one   bone   shell   stone   finally
      I can stay.

Chalcolithic Age

Little copper box I made to hold
the sorrowthings   :   I swallowed it,
keep it from the air's acids. It shines in me.

It is the dawn of *expensive*
and something hardens in there,
something that thinks it lasts.

Simple Machines

My angels, instrumental. My mind let loose
from its bone room, running
among the heavy things, the apart:
> *I want it to go with me.*
> *I want it to hold together.*
> *I want it to rise from the ground.*

Bronze Age

how you make and make a metal skin
how you fasten and keep fastening it
how it is heavy and costly   how it seems
to be everything   how it seems to be
how it always had these gaps
where the birdsound gets in.

Anger: Movement Analysis

It seems to move biologically but just
because it's made of fire   works like plants
do   bloom   stem   root   red
chlorophyll   red milk   red
oxygen   red sugars   photosynthesizes
red light into *just like life.*

Armor: Origin, Constituents, Effects

It happens like skin   it's made
of thought   it feels like *will always be*
will never stop. The cells know what I
don't   where the fighting ends.

Prayer to Hephaestos

Make it so it looks like me but shinier.
Me outlined hard. Build
me out. Keep me bright.

All the Riving

You can say *world's body*   *continuous*
but what about the painline at the skin.
Somebody said *you don't own even that.*

Two Songs

You know the one that goes *I want him still*
  alive. My armor   I need new.
                                  For each something birdlike   *we never*
                                  left   were never anything but what happens.

Process

I confess I love the life of metals   all
the little breakages lining up to process
intransitive   as in a wedding with
an idea of ocean all around.

And What Happens to Armor Then

Eventual's crowbar will pry it off and under
it the body made of asking *what is*
this anyway and world that sound of each
thing answering *what yes what.*

Dream of Running, Troy

I ran past the green/burned/green
and thought *that's my life and its before-
and-after. I used to be other things and
I'll be other things again.* But what
if what I am right now is always other things.

Seawalk, Troy

I picked up a hunk of coral. It's *former*
it's *late*   *it's once I hated you*   *now not*
so much   all calcified pronoun. I set it   the ex-
life of anger and eating and turning what flits
through into hardcoat and calicle   loose. It's just
my day job to know what suffering is.

Simile as Hyperlink

Press here and you're somewhere else. Every
what back home does this remind me of comes
roaring through the rivermouth of then/
now. Just had to tear the fabric a little to
let the singularities in. But there's no way
to use them to find out what will happen afterwards.

Beginning and End of What

My skin replaced itself every
six thoughts. Every two I got
a new picture of things. What is the body
of *all this time*? Something running
all directions until it's not a thing.

Where I'm From

Every day the hardlight called me
armored figure   dry land   but what
about this bit of ocean   inner ear
the sea salt scaffolding   the tiny
swing band at the heart of the
commotion   making waves of everything.

Yes Twice

Yes world came and broke the stick
undid the buckles and what can you say but *consent*
is all my armor now. Armored now in yes.

Made Me

I listened to the clang   rip   stop. Made me
the throughway I've always wanted   always was.

Five Rivers of Yourself

When I fell in   the river said *I'll take*
it from here   the river of your seeing
river of your hearing   river of
your thinking   running   fighting   welcome back.

Is That How

Made of everything's whirl / pour / clatter
is that how this dying got so alive.

Everybody Waves

I've been down this bloodchute before
slaloming the red/black. Fell out
flat on my back against the earth's
calculi   the sky another self
and mine a shotgun road in all
directions. Everybody waves walk-
ing through. God he meant it when he said *I
am the way*. He just meant everybody's I.

What Trace

What I once wanted so badly   a salt
flower back to unbloom on my tongue.
At the x   the cuts where I ran up against
appearing's blades   the juniper's rough
silver bead. Specificity's green needle
in my vein   the visible shushing *been here.*

And To Be Otherwise

I poured down into the sound of the engines cutting
in the cells' red honey   *what's it like*
to be alive and to be otherwise.

Little Song I Heard the Sword Edge Sing

Ungrab the black branch   clay dock.
Knock yourself off and off island.
Be taken   betrothed to not much   whistled
and spun like streetwater. Be unnailed   be
re-unbroken by this breaking   this nail.

Four Ways

Be salt. Be shaken. Be bested
in jousting   in tests. Unenlisted
be swept up in crystals.

Be sugar   the twelfth sister
who hears the diamond-breaker whisper
Oh mastermind   you dissolver in water.

Be the ark's acid shelter
sifter of misfits in lifeboats
its scissors a glitter in matter.

Be the bitter black grass
no one's tasted. Past facts
an unlatching   steadfast   fast.

Delta

Stream A keeps running fulltilt
into B which keeps running. Did
you hear my rivermouth shouting where
I kept   keep   turning into something else.

Not Ever

Let the river   let the dirt   let
the birdsound   let the metals   let the shine
off the hemlocks say what they always say
anyway   *not ever what you think.*

Every Little Iliad

What's breaking/what breaks it make
one life. Because you've got to allow for all
that x that's also self   including the metals.
The cut is where world lets in more world because
there's nothing but. I'll tell you the myth of bounded
things but don't believe it. Rain has no
voice till it stops being rain. *Leaf* then *roof*
is what it can say and isn't that what you'd call
your life   that sound of becoming *else*. How quiet
you have to get to hear the birdsound
of it *here I am here I am here I was.* To sing   to hear
singing   :   to disappear into   disappear as.

Reflection in Moving Water, Troy

I leaned over to look and the water woke
up running. It just means *like this*
and then like this and now like this the self.
It just means *river of this.*

At the Moment of the Dropping Away of the Body, There Is a Voice that Stops All Sound (Or, What Else Became of Me)

A green roar   all that early hydrogen
burning in all those early stars   all
the metallic consequences.

What Interruption

When I say *goldrush* what I mean is how
the gold rushes into itself   how the arrow
that broke me was me   how it keeps going.

Hunk of Ice Sermon

says *thought by thought* is one of those snowballs you toss
on the riverself   the one without pockets to keep.

What Kind of Vow Is That

What you call the palace is running water
the birdsound laughed out loud   studying the little
moment when the water eddied to make my name.

Undoing Lab

Some wind blew through the metal tree   magnetic
nests   the *he injured me irreparably*
model of things. In the undoing lab
you ease up on the grammar of *to settle.*

Slammed

When I slammed down the trees grew
through me except they always had. No
hem   just some rough selvage sewn to
all the other buzzing brightnesses   the body
I'd learned at some point to call *everything else.*

OK Thank You

for seeming to hold still a little long
enough for me to see *her   him*
them. For the three chemical flares that made
me   *Want-it-different. Want. It.*
For me   burning doorway   walking through.

You Asked Me What I Have Now

You know what I have is the sound of it. In fact
that's all I have. In fact I don't even have
that. I'm its roadway. Its road. Its way.

Four Truths, Troy

I was out riding the dirtbike my folks
gave me   front wheel called *bent*
back wheel called *sky*   drinking
that ratty dayglo gatorade you get
in every country store out here. It just
makes you thirsty. So I stopped.
Front wheel said *what next?*
Back wheel said *dunno*.
Even parked the bike is still skimming
somewhere   motor muttering *here's how*.

Night Stroll, Troy

Even as I'm walking its dirt streets
I'm still hungry for it   the world without
its names. *I dreamed I was away love.*
And world said *welcome home anyway.*

River House, Troy

Here's my house of things   a river running
under. House of sounds   a river fills
it up. River joist   lath   vent
say *all water speaking of water.*

And That's How

You make a little bow at the altar of *No Comment* and that's how things flower. All here and that's how you're gone.

Picture a Field Extending

made of *extending*   the door in it made
of swinging. That's one way to love the world.

There Are a Lot of Ways

to love the world   just as so many
trees make my seeing. *I   it*
the glitter of the signal breaking up
the 10K things coming into
going out   that's what makes the shine.

Practice of Three Skies

Field closed up tight and what looked
like sky broke in. The body of any
single thing   some *always* breaking in.

Sky comes down to here and keeps going.
I used to answer when someone called *figure*.
Now I also say yes when someone calls *ground*.

You could call it sky that got into
me. You could call it empty glass
bottle without the glass. But don't make
a thing of it. Don't make a thing.

Where Was I

The river came walking and it was me
walking. The birdsound heard me as itself.
There I was   *I*   in the advent of things.

A Bird Translates Silence

Now that the river's voice has always
been my name

Notes

The epigraph is taken from Eihei Dogen, "The Mountains and Waters Sutra," tr. Shohaku Okumura.

"Subject: Ark Ideation and Prototyping" takes its final sentence from the *Lokka Sutta* ("The World"), tr. Thanissaro Bhikkhu.

"Subject: Glass Box" adapts a phrase from *The Blue Cliff Record* as rendered by Pema Chodron and a line from Eihei Dogen's "Mountain and Waters Sutra," tr. Arnold Kotler and Kazuaki Tanahashi.

"Subject: What Wd It Be To Be Water (We Are Water Divided)" takes its title from Marie Ponsot's 1962 poem "Springing."

"What Kind of Vow Is That" takes its opening phrase from Eihei Dogen, "Mountains and Waters Sutra," tr. Kotler and Tanahashi.

"Angersong" includes a line from *The Derveni Papyrus*, tr. Betegh Gabor.

"Simile as Hyperlink" takes its final sentence from Lee Smolin, *The Life of the Cosmos*.

"Five Rivers of Yourself" takes its title from a phrase in Thich Nhat Hanh's *The Heart of the Buddha's Teaching*.

"At the Moment of the Dropping Away of the Body There is a Voice that Stops All Sound" takes its title from Eihei Dogen, "Body-and-Mind Study of the Way," tr. Kotler and Tanahashi.

In "River House, Troy," the closing phrase is adapted from Eihei Dogen, "Mountains and Waters Sutra," tr. Kotler and Tanahashi.

"A Bird Translates Silence" takes its title from Wong May, "Afterword," *In the Same Light: 200 Poems for Our Century from the Migrants & Exiles of the Tang Dynasty*.

Acknowledgments

Great gratitude to the editors of the publications where these poems first appeared, sometimes under different titles:

Bowery Gothic: "What Interruption," "Slammed," "Where I'm From," "Delta"
Commonweal: "A Lot of Ways"
Green Mountains Review: "Early Things"
The New Yorker: "Subject: Causes and Effects," "Subject: Glass Box"
Pebble Lake Review: "Four Ways"
Still Against War: "Little Song I Heard the Sword Edge Sing," "A Bird Translates Silence," "Where Was I," "Night Stroll, Troy," "Every Little Iliad," "OK Thank You," "Seawalk, Troy"

"To Noah, From Wife" is for DSB, arkmate.
"Rivermouth Shouting" is for Marie Ponsot, hearer of birdsound, everywhere now.

About the Author

Jean Gallagher is the author of *Stubborn*, winner of the FIELD Prize; *This Minute*, winner of the Poets Out Loud Prize; and *Start*. She teaches creative writing at New York University and lives in New York City with her family.

Photograph courtesy of the author.

Free Verse Editions

Edited by Jon Thompson

13 ways of happily by Emily Carr
& in Open, Marvel by Felicia Zamora
& there's you still thrill hour of the world to love by Aby Kaupang
Alias by Eric Pankey
the atmosphere is not a perfume it is odorless by Matthew Cooperman
At Your Feet (A Teus Pés) by Ana Cristina César, edited by
　　Katrina Dodson, trans. by Brenda Hillman and Helen Hillman
Bari's Love Song by Kang Eun-Gyo, translated by Chung Eun-Gwi
Between the Twilight and the Sky by Jennie Neighbors
Blade Work by Lily Brown
Blood Orbits by Ger Killeen
The Bodies by Christopher Sindt
The Book of Isaac by Aidan Semmens
The Calling by Bruce Bond
Canticle of the Night Path by Jennifer Atkinson
Child in the Road by Cindy Savett
Civil Twilight by Giles Goodland
Condominium of the Flesh by Valerio Magrelli, trans. by Clarissa Botsford
Contrapuntal by Christopher Kondrich
Country Album by James Capozzi
Cry Baby Mystic by Daniel Tiffany
The Curiosities by Brittany Perham
Current by Lisa Fishman
Day In, Day Out by Simon Smith
Dear Reader by Bruce Bond
Dismantling the Angel by Eric Pankey
Divination Machine by F. Daniel Rzicznek
Elsewhere, That Small by Monica Berlin
Empire by Tracy Zeman
Erros by Morgan Lucas Schuldt
Extinction of the Holy City by Bronisław Maj, trans. by Daniel Bourne
Field Notes of a Flaneur by Lewis Meyers
Fifteen Seconds without Sorrow by Shim Bo-Seon, trans. by
　　Chung Eun-Gwi and Brother Anthony of Taizé
The Forever Notes by Ethel Rackin
The Flying House by Dawn-Michelle Baude
General Release from the Beginning of the World by Donna Spruijt-Metz

Ghost Letters by Baba Badji
Go On by Ethel Rackin
Here City by Rick Snyder
I Am Not Korean by Song Kyeong-dong
An Image Not a Book by Kylan Rice
Instances: Selected Poems by Jeongrye Choi, trans. by Brenda Hillman,
    Wayne de Fremery, & Jeongrye Choi
Interglacial by Tracy Zeman
Invitatory by Molly Spencer
Last Morning by Simon Smith
The Magnetic Brackets by Jesús Losada, trans. by M. Smith & L. Ingelmo
Man Praying by Donald Platt
A Map of Faring by Peter Riley
The Miraculous Courageous by Josh Booton
Mirrorforms by Peter Kline
M O 月 N by Chengru He
A Myth of Ariadne by Martha Ronk
No Shape Bends the River So Long by Monica Berlin & Beth Marzoni
North | Rock | Edge by Susan Tichy
Not into the Blossoms and Not into the Air by Elizabeth Jacobson
Overyellow, by Nicolas Pesquès, translated by Cole Swensen
Parallel Resting Places by Laura Wetherington
pH of Au by Vanessa Couto Johnson
Physis by Nicolas Pesquès, translated by Cole Swensen
Pilgrimage Suites by Derek Gromadzki
Pilgrimly by Siobhán Scarry
Poems from above the Hill & Selected Work by Ashur Etwebi, trans. by
    Brenda Hillman & Diallah Haidar
The Prison Poems by Miguel Hernández, trans. by Michael Smith
Puppet Wardrobe by Daniel Tiffany
Quarry by Carolyn Guinzio
remanence by Boyer Rickel
Republic of Song by Kelvin Corcoran
Rivermouth Shouting by Jean Gallagher
Rumor by Elizabeth Robinson
Saint with a Peacock Voice by L. S. Klatt
Settlers by F. Daniel Rzicznek
A Short History of Anger by Joy Manesiotis
Signs Following by Ger Killeen
Small Sillion by Joshua McKinney
Split the Crow by Sarah Sousa

www.ingramcontent.com/pod-product-compliance
Lightning Source LLC
Chambersburg PA
CDIIW022039090426
42741CB00007B/1131